THE
GROOVY
GREEKS
ACTIVITY
BOOK

Terry Deary ❧ Martin Brown

SCHOLASTIC

WHO WERE THE GROOVY GREEKS?

The groovy Greeks hung out over 2,000 years ago, from 1600 BC to AD 146, when the rotten Romans took over. These hip 'n' happening Greeks were a mixed bunch – there were horrible heroes, savage Spartans, phoolish philosophers, suffering slaves and ingenious inventors. Their influence is still with us today.

Here's a quick quiz to see how much you know about the groovy Greeks. Simply answer 'Yea' for yes or 'Nay' for no.

WHAT!.. NO DOG FOOD!

1) A slave called Aesop told great stories such as 'The Tortoise and the Hare'. He was richly rewarded by the Greek priests.

2) In the story of Troy, King Agamemnon sacrifices his daughter to the gods. Would that have really happened in ancient Greece?

3) The Greeks read the future using dead birds.

WHAT DO THEY SAY?

IN THE FUTURE THERE WILL BE FEWER BIRDS

4) Hecate was the Greek goddess of crossroads. She would appear with ghosts and phantom dogs. The Greeks left food at crossroads for her.

5) The children who lived in the city of Sparta were super-tough kids. One Spartan boy hid a stolen fox cub under his tunic and didn't let on, even though the fox ate the boy's guts away.

The Greeks were very groovy with numbers. Polybius, born in 200 BC, was a Greek historian of Rome. He is famous for a series of history books that contained 40 volumes, but he also had time to invent this code, now known as Polybius' Checkerboard. Each letter has a pair of numbers – the horizontal (across) number followed by the vertical (up-down). So B is 1-2, but F is 2-1. The word 'Yes' is 54 15 43.

Use the checkerboard to work this out…

44 15 11 13 23 15 42 43　14 34 33'44
25 33 34 52　15 51 15 42 54 44 23 24 33 2
44 23 15 54　24 45 43 44　44 42 54　44 3
25 24 14　54 34 45　44 23 11 44
44 23 15 54　14 34

31 11 44 15　11 22 11 24 33　12 34 54

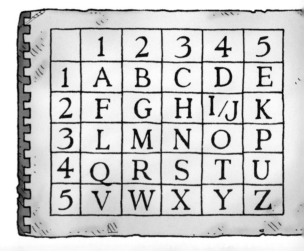

	1	2	3	4	5
1	A	B	C	D	E
2	F	G	H	I/J	K
3	L	M	N	O	P
4	Q	R	S	T	U
5	V	W	X	Y	Z

The Greeks also invented other groovy devices which are still important to us today. One of the cleverest was the camera obscura – or the 'pinhole' camera. A Greek artist covered a window with a dark material, then punched a small hole through. An upside-down image of the scene was seen on the inside wall and traced by the artist. You could have a go at making your own, slightly smaller version.

1) Make a box of black card, 20 x 10 x 10 cm.

2) Make a small pinhole in black paper at one end.

3) Place grease-proof paper across the other end.

4) Hold it up to a bright scene.

5) The scene will be 'projected' on to the grease-proof paper.

Note: this image will be upside-down – you may have to stand on your head to get the best view!

BACK · 20cm · FRONT

GREASE-PROOF PAPER · BLACK PAPER

BLACK BOX · PINHOLE

The Greeks invented some crazy customs for weddings and funerals. Match the right customs to the right events and answer: a wedding, a funeral or both.

1) YOU SHOULD SACRIFICE A LUMP OF YOUR HAIR TO THE GODS BEFORE...
2) YOU SHOULD SHUT THE EYES AND THE MOUTH OF THE MAIN PERSON AT...
3) YOU SHOULD HAVE A TORCH-LIT PROCESSION AT...
4) YOU SHOULD BEAT YOUR HEAD AND TEAR YOUR HAIR AT...
5) YOU SHOULD GIVE THE MAIN PERSON A BATH BEFORE...
6) YOU SHOULD SING AND DANCE AT...
7) YOU SHOULD PLACE A CROWN ON THE HEAD OF THE MAIN PERSON AT...
8) YOU SHOULD THROW FRUIT AND NUTS...
9) YOU SHOULD GIVE GIFTS OF POTTERY, STONE VASES AND MIRRORS AT...
10) YOU SHOULD LEAVE THE PARTY EARLY IF YOU ARE A WOMAN AT...

GRUESOME GODS

The Greeks loved stories, especially horror stories. What about Cronos, chief of the gods? This gruesome god ate his own children. Then eleven babies later, he gave a heavenly heave and threw them all up! The young gods grew to overthrow their dreadful dad. So it was goodbye Cronos – hello Zeus and company.

These new gods were just one big, unhappy family. They were always fighting, arguing and doing horrible things to each other. Can you untangle the names and match the description to each god?

1) SUEZ
Of all the groovy gods, this one was the grooviest. When he wasn't flirting with women, he was frying someone with a thunderbolt.

2) POISONED
Brother to the top god. This sore loser ruled the sea. He stomped around, whipping up the seas with a fork and creating storms. What a stirrer!

3) SHADE
Second brother of the top god and a real loser.
He won the job of ruling the underworld. That must have been hell!

4) A HIRED POT
This lady was the goddess of love and beauty.

5) LOO PAL
This was the sun god and also the god of prophecy.

6) A THANE
The goddess of wisdom and war. What a combination.

A B C D E F

The Greek myths are still popular today – in story books, on television and even at the cinema. They tell of murder, revenge, suffering and lots of death. Test your knowledge and match the sentences below.

1) Paris judged a goddess beauty competition and …

2) Icarus flew too close to the sun and …

3) Cerberus, the three-headed dog …

4) Anyone who looked at Medusa, an ugly snake-haired gorgon …

5) Mighty Atlas became so arrogant that he …

6) When Pandora opened the box she …

a) let out greed and envy, hatred and cruelty, poverty and hunger, sickness and despair.

b) was doomed to stand forever, bearing the weight of the world.

c) guarded the entrance to Hades, or hell.

d) melted the wax on his wings.

e) turned to stone.

f) gave the winner a golden apple.

FIGHT LIKE A GREEK

Groovy Greeks loved stories about heroes – men who were almost as powerful as gods. There was a snag … they were mortal and so could die. Stories about heroes were told as poems and sung in the ancient palaces of Greece. Later, they were written down. The oldest poem was by the writer Homer, who wrote an epic poem called The Iliad, all about the siege of Troy. Heroes fought to the death to get the most beautiful woman in the world, Helen, back to hubby, King Menelaus.

Everyone knows the story of the wooden horse of Troy. But can you believe it? Put these pictures in the correct order to read what happened when those Trojan twits saw a wooden horse standing outside the gates of the city.

I — OH, ALL RIGHT. LOOK, IT EVEN HAS WHEELS ON TO MAKE IT EASY

E — I'VE GOT A GREAT IDEA. WHY DON'T WE BRING IT INSIDE THE CITY. WE CAN HAVE IT AS A SORT OF STATUE IN THE CENTRE OF THE CITY

G — OOOOH! LOOK! A WOODEN HORSE / WHAT'S IT DOING HERE?

A — JUST TO SHOW THERE'S NO HARD FEELINGS, I SUPPOSE / IT'LL LOOK VERY NICE THERE OUTSIDE THE WALLS

F — NAH! YOUR MOTHER NEVER TRUSTED NOBODY. 'ERE, GRAB THAT ROPE AND GIVE US A HAND

D — ER … PARIS, YOU DON'T THINK THIS COULD BE SOME SORT OF … WELL … TRICK, DO YOU? MUMMY DID SAY 'BEWARE THE GREEKS BEARING GIFTS'

H — THAT'S KIND OF THEM. THEY SPEND TEN YEARS TRYING TO MURDER US THEN GO OFF AND LEAVE US A PRESENT...

C — THE GREEKS MUST HAVE LEFT IT / WHY? / DUNNO. MAYBE IT'S A PREZZIE

J — ALMOST AS IF THE GREEKS WANTED US TO TAKE IT INTO THE CITY / THOUGHTFUL OF THEM. VERY THOUGHTFUL

B — NOT A LOT OF WOODEN STATUES ABOUT / WE'LL BE THE FIRST. START A NEW FASHION

Correct order of pictures:

King Darius of Persia had a large army and decided it was about time he took over Greece. The Greeks wouldn't have feared the Persians so much if they knew what the great historian Herodotus knew. He told a remarkable story about an earlier Persian battle at Pelusium in Egypt...

On the battlefield I saw a strange thing which the natives pointed out to me. The bones of the dead lay scattered on the field in two lots – those of the Persians and those of the Egyptians. If, then, you strike a Persian skull, they are so weak you will break a hole in them. But the Egyptian skulls are so strong that you may hit them with a rock and hardly crack them.

Count how many Persian and Egyptian skulls you can see in this picture to see who won.

Can you work out which of these things were first seen in ancient Greece.

1) SOAP
2) CAMERA
3) PARACHUTE
4) ANCHOR
5) CHEWING GUM
6) SIREN
7) CATAPULT
8) SANDWICHES
9) ROLLER SKATES
10) SPECTACLES

SAVAGE SPARTANS

**The Spartans were the toughest of all the Greeks.
They believed they were better than anyone else. If they wanted more
land then they just moved into someone else's patch. If someone was
already living there the Spartans just made them slaves. In short,
they were the ungrooviest lot in the whole of Greece.**

*Life was extra-tough for Spartan kids. Add the missing words to
read these strict Spartan rules.*

MISSING WORDS NOT IN THE CORRECT ORDER: mountains, hair, herd, bite, baths, no clothes, beaten.

1) A child belongs to the state of Sparta. At the age of seven, children will join a _____.

2) A bad serving-child will receive a _____ on the back of the hand.

3) A sickly baby will be taken to the _____.

4) A new bride must cut off her _____ and dress like a man.

5) Children caught stealing food will be _____.

6) A Spartan child may have only a few _____ a year.

7) In processions, dances and temple services, girls must wear _____.

> THAT THASOS IS A CLEANLINESS FREAK

> YEAH... THAT'S HIS THIRD BATH THIS YEAR

*One Spartan general wanted to betray his country. But things didn't quite go
to plan. Unscramble the words in CAPITAL LETTERS to read the story.
The number in brackets tells you where the words should go in the grid.
The blue column will tell you the name of this sly Spartan.*

One great Spartan general helped to FATEED (2)
the Persians in 479 BC. But the Spartans thought he was
getting too big-headed. He was asked to return to
STARAP (1) to be UPDISHEN (3). The general was
not happy. He wrote to the Persian NIKG (6), Xerxes,
and offered to betray Sparta. The nosy messenger
opened the letter to find a deadly 'Ps – LIKL (7)
the messenger!' So, the messenger took it back to Sparta,
and they sent a force to kill the RATTIOR (5). The
general fled to a temple in Athena, but the SISNSASAS
(4) bricked up the door and starved him to death. Later,
the general's THOGS (9) came back to THUNA (8)
the temple. In the end, the priestess sent for a magician –
a sort of groovy Greek ghostbuster – to get rid of him.

Spartans lied, cheated and tricked their way out of trouble. If this didn't work, they died fighting. King Leonidas led 300 Spartans to defend Thermopylae against tens of thousands of Persians. The Persian leader, Xerxes, couldn't believe the Spartans would be daft enough to fight and die. Xerxes didn't know the Spartans. Look at the two battle scenes below. Spot ten differences between the two and circle them with a pencil.

LIVE LIKE A GREEK

Athens, being really groovy, had the first democracy. This is a society where every adult has a vote on laws and how money is spent. But because the Greeks still had a lot to learn, they didn't quite get it right! Everyone had the vote except women, poor people, anyone under 30 years and slaves. So, ancient Greece wasn't as perfect as they liked to think.

Being a female in ancient Greece wasn't much fun. They were told what to do and what not to do – they didn't have the freedom that the men enjoyed (those that weren't slaves that is). Which of the following statements are true and which are false?

1) A WOMAN MAY BUY OR SELL ANYTHING THAT IS WORTH MORE THAN A SMALL MEASURE OF BARLEY.

2) A WOMAN MUST LEARN TO SPIN, WEAVE, COOK AND MANAGE SLAVES.

3) A WOMAN MUST WORSHIP THE GODDESS HESTIA.

4) A WOMAN MUST BE BROUGHT UP WITH SLAVES AND LEARN HOUSEHOLD SKILLS.

5) A WOMAN MUST STAY AT HOME.

6) A WOMAN MAY OWN THINGS OTHER THAN HER CLOTHES, JEWELLERY AND SLAVES.

7) A WOMAN OUGHT TO HAVE A HUSBAND (CHOSEN BY HER FATHER) WHEN SHE IS 15.

8) A WOMAN MUST NOT GO OUT EXCEPT TO VISIT OTHER WOMEN OR TO GO TO RELIGIOUS FESTIVALS, WEDDINGS AND FUNERALS.

9) A WOMAN MAY ALLOW ANYONE TO VISIT WITHOUT HER HUSBAND KNOWING.

10) A WOMAN MAY VOTE.

FEMALE? FEMALE? NO FEMALES HERE! JUST US BLOKES

Life was even worse for slaves. Alexandria was a city in Egypt ruled by the Greeks. Around 250 BC they had a set of rules which help us to understand how Greek law worked. Can you match the crime to the punishment?

1) A free man strikes another free man or free woman.

2) A slave strikes a free man or free woman.

3) A drunk person injures someone else.

4) A free man threatens another with wood, iron or bronze.

5) A slave threatens another with wood, iron or bronze.

a) Fine of 100 drachmas.

b) Fine of 200 drachmas.

c) A hundred lashes.

d) A hundred lashes.

e) Fine of 100 drachmas.

From 500–200 BC, the Greeks had a ruthless way of treating babies. Follow the steps below to see if you would have made a good parent in ancient Greece.

START

Father inspects baby. Is it fit?

YES Go to 1.
NO Go to 2.
DON'T KNOW Go to 5

1

If you have too many boys then they'll have to split up your land when you die. Too many girls will cost you money. Do you want to keep it?

YES Go to 6.
NO Go to 2.

2

Put the baby in a pot (a pithos), then leave baby on a hillside to die. Do you care?

YES Go to 4.
NO Go to 3.

3

Baby dies before it's a week old.

4

Let a childless couple know what's going on. They will get to it before the cold or the wolves do. Baby lives with foster parents.

Go to 6.

5

Father will 'test' the baby by rubbing it with icy water, wine or urine (yeuch). Does it survive?

YES Go to 6.
NO Go to 3.

6

The baby is one of the family. Tell the world with an olive branch on the door if it's a boy, a piece of wool for a girl.

GO to 7.

7

Hold the Amphidromia ceremony. When baby is seven days old, sweep the house and sprinkle it with water. Father holds baby and runs round hearth with it while family sing hymns.

GO to 8.

8

When baby is ten days old, have the naming ceremony. (A boy is named after his grandfather.) Congratulations — you've made it … unless disease, plague or war or something else gets you!

GROOVY GREEK GAMES

The Groovy Greeks liked nothing better than a contest. The first Olympic games were simple foot races, around 776 BC. The first few Olympics had just one race on one day – a race of about 190 metres or the length of the stadium. Other longer races were added over the years until the meeting lasted five days. There was even a junior Olympics for kids!

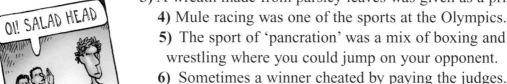

Here's a quick quiz to see how much you know about the groovy Olympics. Simply answer 'Yea' for yes or 'Nay' for no.

1) When the winners got home they were given free haircuts as extra rewards.

2) At the first Olympic games the winner was given a cauldron as a prize.

3) A wreath made from parsley leaves was given as a prize.

4) Mule racing was one of the sports at the Olympics.

5) The sport of 'pancration' was a mix of boxing and wrestling where you could jump on your opponent.

6) Sometimes a winner cheated by paying the judges. If he was caught the winner could lose the title.

7) The Greeks had their own names for their contests. One of the games was called hoplitodromos.

8) The spoilsport Romans came along and banned the Olympics in AD 394.

OI! SALAD HEAD

I THINK I PREFER THE TROJAN WAR

Can you find these words listed in the puzzle? The words can be found written forwards or backwards. Then unscramble the letters that are left to work out the name of the goddess of victory, who watched over all athletic contests.

ARENA, BATON, CHAMPION, CHARIOT, COMPETITION, CROWN, GYMNASIUM, HORSE, JAVELIN, OLYMPICS, PANCRATION, PRIZE, RACE, RELAY, SPORT, TEAM, TORCH, WRESTLER

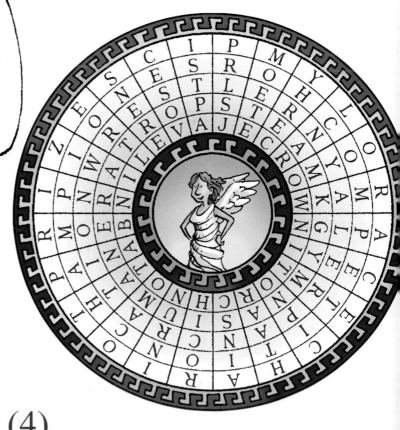

GODDESS _ _ _ _ (4)

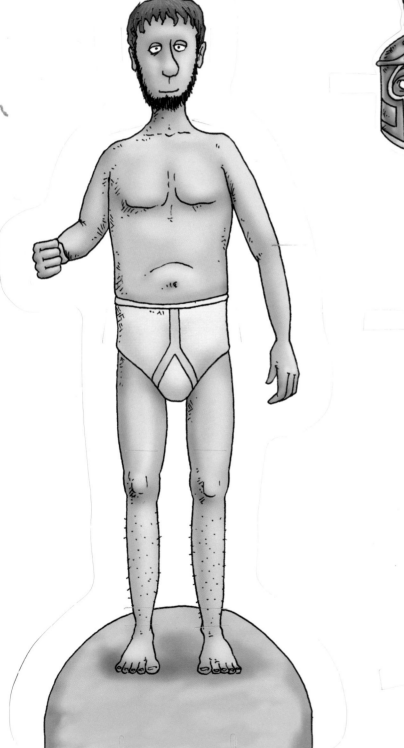

Push the pieces out of the card and choose the correct armour and weapons to dress your own general and foot soldier. Yes, we know Greeks didn't wear underpants – but you didn't want to see him with nothing on, did you? Turn to the inside of the back cover to see these groovy Greeks ready for battle.

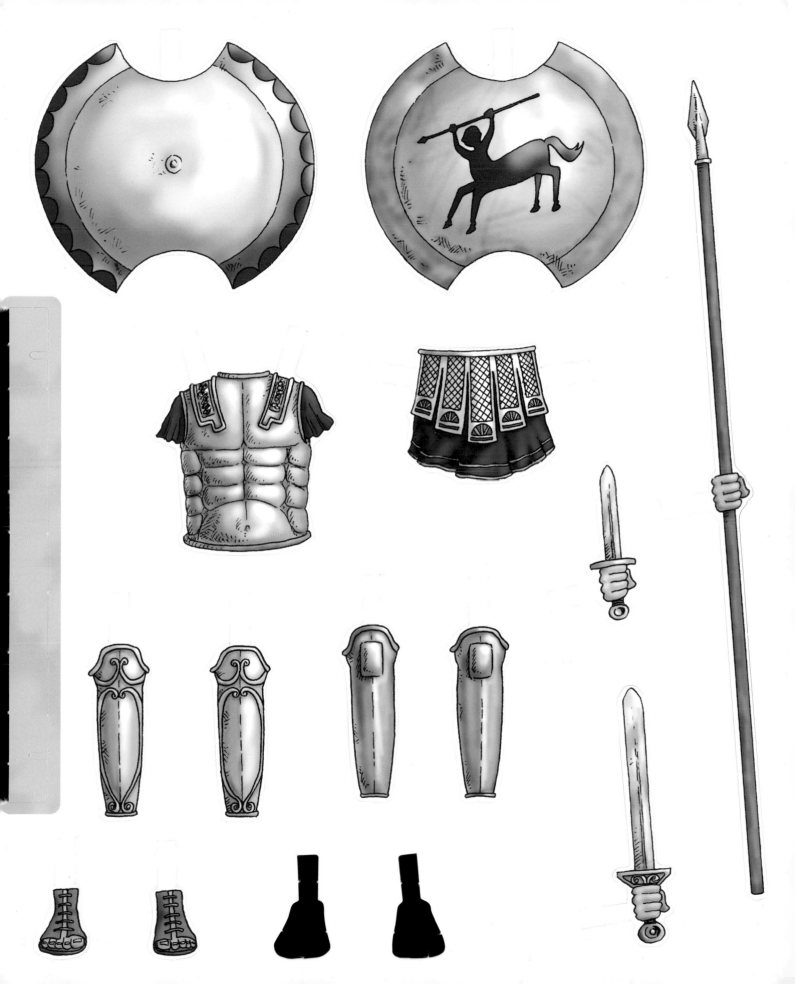

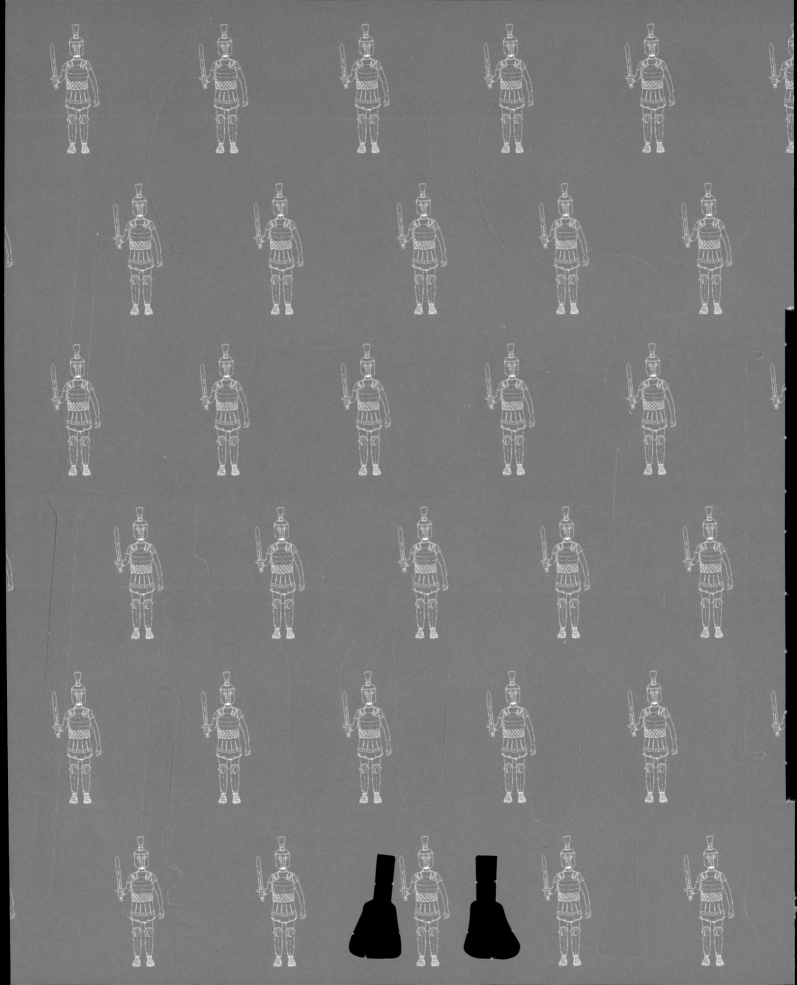

1. Champion wrestler, Timanthese, lost his strength. He was so upset he did what?

a) He built a tower and threw himself off the top.

b) He built a fire and threw himself into it.

c) He built a pond and drowned himself in it.

I'M NOT TAKING ANY CHANCES

2. Handsome Creugas and big bully Damoxenos fought to a standstill in a boxing match. The referee said they could each have one free shot at the other. Damoxenos killed Creugas with a cheat. What did he do?

a) He pulled a knife out of his hair band and stabbed Creugas.

b) He borrowed a nearby javelin and speared Creugas.

c) He used his sharp fingernails to rip Creugas's belly open and then pulled out his guts.

I'M GUTTED!

3. The Olympics were supposed to have started when King Oeomaus said to young Pelops, 'You want to marry my daughter? Then race me in a chariot.' Pelops won when King Oeomaus died. How?

a) Pelops nobbled Oeomaus's chariot.

b) Pelops nobbled Oeomaus's horses.

c) Pelops nobbled Oeomaus's drink.

4. Wrestler Milo won five Olympic games as a wrestler and was super-strong. (He once held up the collapsing roof of a building while people escaped.) But he died when he tried his strength against what?

a) a lion

b) a tree

c) a woman

TICKLE TICKLE TICKLE

5. Wrestler Polydamas was another super-strong man. He once held a fierce bull so firmly it had to tear its own hoof off to escape. (Yeuch!) How did his strength finish him off?

a) He tried to copy Milo by holding up a collapsing roof.

b) He tried to copy Greek god Heracles by fighting a lion with his bare hands.

c) He tried to copy his old trick of ripping off a bull's hoof.

EVEN GROOVIER GREEK GAMES

You didn't have to be an athlete to enjoy games. Greek children invented games that are still played in some parts of the world today. In fact, you may have played some of the games yourself. If you haven't, and want to play like a groovy Greek, then here are some of the best.

The Greeks played ball games where you throw a ball at a 'wicket', rather like cricket without a batsman. We have pictures of these games that have been painted on Greek vases, but we don't have their rules. Maybe they played like this…

Greecket

1) Stand on a mark a fixed distance from the wicket.
2) Take a ball and have ten attempts to hit the wicket.
3) Your opponent stands behind the wicket (like a wicket-keeper) and throws the ball back to you every time.
4) Then you stand behind the wicket while your opponent tries.
5) The one who has the most hits on the wicket from ten throws is the winner. It looks (from the vase paintings) as if the loser has to give the winner a piggy-back ride!

WHY IS IT ALWAYS THE BIG KIDS WHO ARE GOOD AT GAMES?

Bronze Fly

This game is a sort of Greek Blind-man's Buff. A Greek described it…

THEY FASTENED A HEADBAND ROUND A BOY'S EYES. HE TURNED ROUND AND ROUND AND CALLED OUT, 'I WILL CHASE THE BRONZE FLY!' THE OTHERS CALLED BACK, 'YOU MIGHT CHASE HIM BUT YOU WON'T CATCH HIM.' THEY THEN TORMENT HIM WITH PAPER WHIPS UNTIL HE CATCHES ONE OF THEM.

ISN'T THAT A BULL WHIP?

NOT VERY GOOD ARE YOU?

Kottabos

To play this game, you will need a cup of water and a 50p coin on the end of a broom handle. Even grown-up Greeks played this silly game with wine at parties.
1) Take a broom handle and stand it upright.
2) Balance a 50p on top of the pole.
3) Grip the cup of water by the handle.
4) Flick the water out and try to knock the coin off the top of the pole.

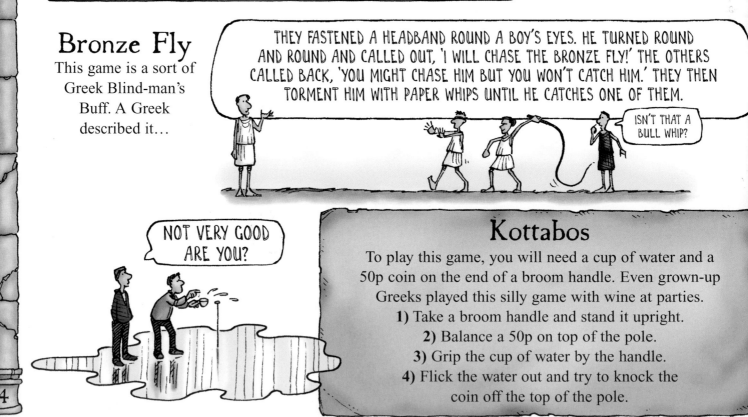

14

In the game called Ephedrismos, a player was blindfolded and gave someone a piggy-back. The rider had to guide the player to a target. This would have been a competition where pairs of players raced to reach the target. Can you work out which path will lead the players to the target?

START

FINISH

DIE LIKE A GREEK

The first Greek doctors didn't work from a hospital, they worked from a temple. The temple was famous because no one ever died there. The doctor-priests cheated. If someone was dying when they arrived then they weren't allowed in. And if they started dying once they got inside, they were dumped in the nearby woods.

Hippocrates was a Greek doctor who believed in the proper study of the body using experiments. Hippocrates also had advice for doctors. He obviously took it – he lived until he was 99! Read the text, then find the words in CAPITALS in the wordsearch. The words are written forwards, backwards, up, down, diagonally and across.

Hippo took samples from his patients and tested them. But he couldn't test them in a laboratory with chemicals the way modern doctors can. He tested them by tasting them or making his patient taste them. Which of the following horrible things were tasted to test? Answer 'Yummy yes' or 'Nasty no'.

A DOCTOR must be careful not to get too FAT. Someone who can't look after his own FITNESS shouldn't be allowed to look after other people's. Secondly, he should be CLEAN, wear good CLOTHES and use a sweet (but not too strong) SCENT. This is pleasant when visiting the SICK. He must not look too grim or too cheerful – a GRIM man will worry the PATIENT while a laughing man may be seen as an IDIOT.

A	O	C	S	S	E	N	T	I	F
H	I	C	L	O	T	H	E	S	O
O	A	R	D	E	I	O	C	P	R
I	D	I	O	T	A	I	D	A	G
R	F	A	N	P	Q	N	S	T	C
O	M	I	R	G	L	T	R	I	S
T	A	P	A	T	E	N	O	E	K
C	F	O	S	N	L	E	P	N	C
O	L	T	T	D	O	C	R	T	I
D	B	T	A	F	E	S	S	A	S

1) TOENAILS
2) VOMIT
3) HAIR
4) EAR WAX
5) PUS FROM INFECTED WOUNDS
6) TEARS
7) SKIN
8) SNOT
9) SPIT
10) PEE

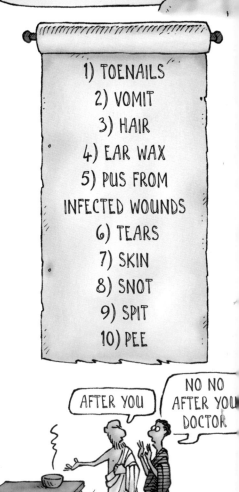

AFTER YOU

NO NO AFTER YOU DOCTOR

Not every doctor was as good as Hippocrates. King Pyrrhus of Greece had a deadly doctor in 278 BC. The doc wrote to the Romans and said he was willing to poison the Greek king if they paid him. But the Romans sent the letter straight back to Pyrrhus to tell him there was a traitor in his camp – they didn't want to be blamed for the murder. Can you lead the messenger back to the Greek camp before the doctor does the deadly deed?

FUNNY FOOD

One historian said, 'The Greeks had meals of two courses; the first a kind of porridge – and the second a kind of porridge.' It wasn't quite that bad. You'd find much more at a groovy Greek meal. Peasants liked olives, figs, nuts or goat's milk cheese. As time went by, the diet got richer, and the rich started to eat more and more meat. Roast goat was a particular favourite.

A sacrifice is supposed to be a groovy gift to the gods. When the Greeks sacrificed an animal to a god, they roasted it and they ate it. That's a bit like buying your mum a box of chocolates then scoffing them yourself. Answer the questions below to find out more about the Greek's gruesome eating habits.

1. At a sacrifice, the greatest honour was to eat:
a) roasted heart, lungs, liver or kidney
b) the tail
c) the chargilled eyeballs

2. What did the Greeks leave behind for the gods?
a) tail, thigh bones and gall bladder
b) nothing
c) skin

3. Greeks mixed the blood and fat together and stuffed it into the bladder of an animal. People these days ask for this at the butchers – what is it?
a) haggis
b) black pudding
c) sausage

4. There was no sugar in those days. How did the ancient Greeks sweeten their food?
a) crushed grapes
b) herbs
c) honey

5. Vegetarians in ancient Greece sacrificed:
a) vegetables
b) cows that had died of old age
c) sticks

6. The Spartans had a disgusting concoction called Black Broth. It was made from:
a) fish guts
b) mixed pork juices, salt and vinegar
c) calf's feets and vegetables

7. Aristotle, the great Greek teacher, had a favourite meat. What was it?
a) camel
b) turkey
c) horse liver

After about 500 BC, the rich started to eat meat – goat, mutton, pork and deer. But they also had a taste for some unusual food. Unscramble the words to read what food is on the menu. Then decide which foods the ancient Greeks would and wouldn't have eaten.

WHAT A PIG!

1) SHE HURTS
2) DEEP FROGS IV
3) SAUCER SHIN
4) ODDER HIKING SYRUP
5) SOCK CAGE PEG
6) YAK SCENE HO
7) SPURN IT
8) OWLES FEEREDS
9) PERHAPS GROSS
10) TIGHT PEAS

Milon was a wrestler. He was also a very greedy Greek. Read the story below. Then find the words in CAPITALS in the wordsearch. The words are written forwards, backwards, up, down and diagonally.

Milon thought he was pretty groovy. Before one OLYMPIC contest he walked around a STADIUM with a live young BULL on his SHOULDERS. Then, he KILLED the bull and ate it. He finished the whole bull before the day was out. The GODS decided to teach him a LESSON. It happened when Milon was showing off again. He SPLIT open a tree with his hands ... but they became stuck in the split. Try as he might he couldn't get free. When a pack of WOLVES came along they licked their chops and moved in on Milon. What do you think they did to Milon? Just what Milon did to the young bull – except they probably didn't COOK him first.

NIBBLE NIBBLE NIBBLE

S	D	E	L	L	I	K	O	C
R	D	H	A	E	L	O	L	H
E	C	O	O	S	I	O	Y	O
D	U	H	G	S	K	C	M	S
L	S	C	A	O	R	Y	P	E
U	I	P	F	N	S	T	I	V
O	D	K	L	P	D	Q	C	L
H	T	L	O	I	Y	S	G	O
S	U	H	T	O	T	W	I	W
B	C	M	U	I	D	A	T	S

THINK LIKE A GREEK

The Greeks had some of the cleverest thinkers of ancient times. Yet they had some very strange beliefs. They were very superstitious and believed in horoscopes, ghosts and gods deciding their fate. They believed that the gods spoke through 'Oracles', a priest or priestess, and you could learn about the future…

At the Corinth Oracle, you could speak directly to a god. You spoke to the alter … and a voice boomed back. Visitors believed it was a miracle. The truth is, a secret tunnel led under the alter. A priest crawled through the tunnel. He listened to the speaker and answered through a tube. Can you find your way through this maze to the cheating priest?

People today are nervous about walking under a ladder because they think it will bring them bad luck, or they touch wood to bring them good luck. The Greeks had their own strange superstitions. Fill in the missing words to read about what they believed…

Missing words not in the correct order: messengers, wickedness, earth, moon, spirits, protected, evil, bodies, dead, disease, tar, reflection, die

I WISH THEY'D SEND SHORTER MESSAGES

1) Birds were _____ between _____ and heaven, and the _____ was a resting place for spirits on their way to heaven.

2) Some Greeks kept dead _____ in jars called pithos. But sometimes, they said, the spirits of the _____ escaped from the jars and began to bother the living with illness and _____. The best way to stop the wicked spirits from getting into your house was to paint _____ round the door frames.

3) The Greeks believed that if you dreamed about seeing your _____ in a mirror then you would _____ soon after.

4) Greeks thought there were _____ called 'daimons' around. Some were good and _____ you; some were _____ and could lead you into _____.

IT WASN'T ME SIR, IT WAS MY DAIMON

Can you imagine your maths teacher setting up his own religion? This is what the famous teacher, Pythagoras, did. He and his followers lived apart from the rest of the Greek people and had some rather strange beliefs. Read these ridiculous rules and decide which ones are true and which ones are false.

1) DON'T EAT BEANS.

2) DON'T EAT THE HEART OF AN ANIMAL.

3) DON'T LOOK IN A MIRROR BESIDE A LAMP.

4) DON'T WALK ALONG THE MAIN STREET.

5) DON'T TOUCH A WHITE COCKEREL.

ALL I DID WAS ASK HIM TO HELP ME MOVE THESE WHITE COCKERELS

6) DON'T STAND ON YOUR FINGERNAIL CLIPPINGS.

How many of the following facts can you rearrange into the right order.

1) The Greek explorer, Pytheas,	ran about naked in the woods	his dead mother's coffin
2) The Greek teacher, Gorgias,	trained in	hockey
3) Spartan youths	cut off a girl's head	on the statues of Greek gods
4) A Greek sportsman	was born in	the North Sea
5) The girls of Attica	enjoyed the team sport called	you shouldn't touch a fire with an iron poker
6) The Greek teacher, Pythagoras,	believed	pretending to be bears
7) The Greek doctor, Aesculapius,	knocked off the naughty bits	to cure water on the brain
8) General Alcibiades	sailed to	the secret police

GROOVY GREEK QUIZ

So you think you know a thing or two about the groovy Greeks? Test your knowledge with this multiple choice quiz and see if you're a true Greek expert or not.

1. The great playwright, Aeschylus, is supposed to have died when an eagle flew over his head and dropped something on it. What did the eagle drop?

a) a tortoise

b) a hare

c) a stone

2. What is a Doric Chiton?

a) a sharp knife

b) an early kite made out of papyrus and hemp

c) a type of tunic

3. The Greeks invented a new weapon in the 4th century BC. They set fire to inflammable liquids then threw them over enemy ships or enemy cities. What is this weapon called?

a) Greek fire

b) Zeus's revenge

c) flaming dangerous

4. A sacred plant was sprinkled on graves. We don't consider it sacred today. What is it?

a) cabbage

b) parsley

c) garlic

5. What did the Greek gods eat?

a) ambrosia

b) ancient Greeks

c) aubergines

6. As well as the Olympic games, there were games in Isthmia. The winners at the Isthmian games were given a crown as a prize. What was the crown made of?

a) rhubarb

b) celery

c) gold

7. The Greek god of wine and merry-making was the grooviest god of all. What was his name?

a) Didymus

b) Dionysus

c) Dipymus

8. Draco wrote the first law books for the Athenians. Which statement is true?

a) You could have someone made your personal slave if they owed you money.

b) If you stole an apple or a cabbage, you were sentenced to death.

c) People found guilty of idleness would be executed.

9. Before clever Aristotle came along, the Greeks had a strange belief about elephants. What was it?

a) An elephant has no knee joints so it goes to sleep leaning against a tree.

b) Elephants never forget.

c) Eating elephant makes you strong.

10. The poet Homer, described a race between Achilles and Odysseus (who was losing). He said a prayer to Athena who made Achilles slip and fall into...

a) cattle droppings

b) a puddle

c) a hole in the ground

ANSWER PAGES

PAGES 2-3: WHO WERE THE GROOVY GREEKS?

Here's a quick quiz to see...

1 = NAY   2 = YEA   3 = YEA   4 = YEA   5 = YEA
1) They threw him off the top of a cliff.
2) Not only were children sacrificed, but bits of them were eaten, too.
5) This was a popular story told by Spartans. It was probably one big fib.

The Greeks were very groovy with...

Teachers don't know everything, they just try to kid you that they do.

The Greeks invented some crazy customs...

1 = BOTH   2 = A FUNERAL   3 = BOTH   4 = A FUNERAL
5 = BOTH   6 = BOTH   7 = BOTH   8 = A WEDDING
9 = BOTH   10 = A FUNERAL

PAGES 4-5: GRUESOME GODS

These new gods were just one...

1 = ZEUS = E   2 = POSEIDON = C   3 = HADES = A
4 = APHRODITE = D   5 = APOLLO = B   6 = ATHENA = F

The Greek myths are still popular today...

1 = f   2 = d   3 = c   4 = e   5 = b   6 = a

PAGES 6-7: FIGHT LIKE A GREEK

Everyone knows the story of...

Correct order of pictures: G, C, H, A, E, B, I, J, D, F

King Darius of Persia had a large...

16 Persian skulls   123 Egyptian skulls.
The Persians won the battle at Pelusium.

Can you work out which of these things...

1) SOAP = YES   2) CAMERA = NO   3) PARACHUTE = NO
4) ANCHOR = YES   5) CHEWING GUM = YES   6) SIREN = YES
7) CATAPULT = YES   8) SANDWICHES = NO
9) ROLLER SKATES = NO   10) SPECTACLES = NO
1) Made from goat fat and ashes.
2) Invented in Britain in the 1820's and 30's.
3) First jump was made from a hot air balloon in Britain, 1797.
5) The ancient Greeks chewed mastic gum – resin from the bark of the
   mastic tree, found mainly in Greece and Turkey. Used to clean their
   teeth and sweeten their breath.
8) The Romans first had the idea of eating meat between bread.
9) First seen in 1700's Britain. Joseph Merlin skated into a ballroom,
   playing a violin.
10) Invented around 1287 in Italy.

PAGES 8-9: SAVAGE SPARTANS

Life was extra-tough for Spartan...

1 = herd   2 = bite   3 = mountains   4 = hair
5 = beaten   6 = baths   7 = no clothes
1) The toughest child became leader and ordered the others about.
3) Sickly babies were left up a mountain to die.
5) Children were kept hungry and encouraged to steal food!
7) So they didn't get fancy ideas about fine clothes.

One Spartan general wanted to betray his...

1 = SPARTA   2 = DEFEAT   3 = PUNISHED
4 = ASSASSINS   5 = TRAITOR   6 = KING
7= KILL   8 = HAUNT   9 = GHOST
The Spartan general was called PAUSANIUS.

Spartans lied, cheated and tricked their way...

PAGES 10-11: LIVE LIKE A GREEK

Being a female in ancient Greece...

1 = FALSE   2 = TRUE   3 = TRUE   4 = TRUE   5 = TRUE
6 = FALSE   7 = TRUE   8 = TRUE   9 = FALSE   10 = FALSE

Life was even worse for...

1 = a   2 = c   3 = b   4 = e   5 = d

PAGES 12-13: GROOVY GREEK GAMES

Here's a quick quiz to see how much...

1 = NAY   2 = YEA   3 = YEA   4 = YEA
5 = YEA   6 = NAY   7 = YEA   8 = YEA
1) They were given a pension, free meals and money.
6) They could be whipped or banned from future games.
7) This was a race in armour.

Can you find the words...

NIKE was the goddess of victory.

Not all Olympic champs died...

1 = b   2 = c   3 = a   4 = b   5 = a

PAGES 14-15: EVEN GROOVIER GREEK GAMES

In the game called…

PAGES 16-17: DIE LIKE A GREEK

Hippocrates was a…

Hippo took samples…

1 = Nasty no
2 = Yummy yes
3 = Nasty no
4 = Yummy yes
5 = Yummy yes
6 = Yummy yes
7 = Nasty no
8 = Yummy yes
9 = Nasty no
10 = Yummy yes

Not every doctor was as good as…

PAGES 18-19: FUNNY FOOD

A sacrifice is supposed to be…

1 = a   2 = a   3 = b   4 = c   5 = a   6 = b   7 = a

After about 500 BC…

1 = THRUSHES
2 = OVERFED PIGS
3 = SEA URCHINS
4 = YORKSHIRE PUDDING
5 = PEACOCK EGGS
6 = HONEY CAKES
7 = TURNIPS
8 = FLOWER SEEDS
9 = GRASSHOPPERS
10 = SPAGHETTI

The Greeks would have eaten them all except 4 and 10.

Milon was a wrestler…

PAGES 20-21: THINK LIKE A GREEK

At the Corinth Oracle…

People today are nervous about…

Missing words in the correct order: messengers, earth, moon, bodies, dead, disease, tar, reflection, die, spirits, protected, evil, wickedness.

Can you imagine your maths…

ALL TRUE!

How many of the following facts…

1) The Greek explorer, Pytheas, sailed to the North Sea.
2) The Greek teacher, Gorgias, was born in his dead mother's coffin.
3) Spartan youths trained in the secret police.
4) A Greek sportsman enjoyed the team sport called hockey.
5) The girls of Attica ran about naked in the woods pretending to be bears.
6) The Greek teacher, Pythagoras, believed you shouldn't touch a fire with an iron poker.
7) The Greek doctor, Aesculapius, cut off a girl's head to cure water on the brain.
8) General Alcibiades knocked off the naughty bits on the statues of Greek gods.

PAGE 22: GROOVY GREEK QUIZ

1 = a   2 = c   3 = a   4 = b   5 = a
6 = b   7 = b   8 = a, b and c   9 = a   10 = a

Scholastic Children's Books,
Commonwealth House, 1–19 New Oxford Street,
London WC1A 1NU, UK
A division of Scholastic Ltd
London ~ New York ~ Toronto ~ Auckland ~
Sydney ~ Mexico City ~ New Delhi ~ Hong Kong
Published in the UK by Scholastic Ltd, 2004
Some of the material in this book has previously
been published in Horrible Histories:
The Groovy Greeks and *The Awesome
Ancient Quiz Book.*

Text copyright © Terry Deary, 1996, 2001
Illustrations copyright © Martin Brown, 1996-2001
All rights reserved

ISBN 0 439 96291 9

2 4 6 8 10 9 7 5 3 1

The right of Terry Deary and Martin Brown to be
identified as the author and illustrator of this work
respectively has been asserted by them in
accordance with the Copyright, Designs and
Patents Act, 1988.

Additional material by Pam Kelt
Additional illustrations and colour work by
Mike Phillips and Stuart Martin

Created and produced by The Complete Works,
St Mary's Road, Royal Leamington Spa,
Warwickshire CV31 1JP, UK

Printed and bound
by Tien Wah Press Pte. Ltd, Singapore